I0004954

The Complete Handbook

On Using Windows 10

Introduction

Earlier this year on July 29th of 2015, Windows released what has been deemed a familiar operating system with great new features to match modern day usage – Windows 10. Microsoft even allows existing Windows 7 and 8 users to upgrade for free– something many people find to be quite beneficial. However, the steps that come after installing a new operating system can cause some concern for people. How much has changed? Will you be able to understand the changes? What do you really need to know? Though there are many answers to those questions, there are always key points to address in any operating system upgrade. So if you are one of the many people looking for an upgrade on an existing piece of technology (PC laptop or desktop, tablet) that already runs Windows, this book offers tips and important information from the start of the process until the moment you are ready to take off on your own and enjoy.

Chapter One: Upgrade & First Steps

As mentioned in the introduction, the upgrade to Windows 10 is completely free so long as you already have Windows 7 or 8 already running on your machine. Though it may vary whether you are upgraded to Windows 10 Home or Windows 10 Pro based off your current program, in this chapter we will cover the basics. So how can you go about doing your upgrade yourself? It is quite simple, really!

One option is to stop by a Microsoft Store, or a store offering Microsoft services, for the upgrade. However, you can also opt to download and install the upgrade yourself. As this is a free upgrade offered by Microsoft, you will need to go to their website to begin. Make sure you have a stable and fast internet connection before getting started! You would not want your internet to go out in the middle of the download or eat up hours of your day.

1. Check your stats. Be sure you have enough data storage and your PC or tablet meet the minimum system requirements for the upgrade. These can be found listed on the Microsoft website.
2. Go to the main Microsoft website.
3. Navigate to software downloads and select the Windows 10 upgrade.
4. Once the program is finished downloading, begin the installation process. A window that will launch a series of screens with information will prompt this. Click 'next' on each to proceed and follow the instructions.

First Step: Privacy Set Up

Now that you have successfully upgraded to Windows 10, there are so many things at your fingertips, you may not even know where to get started. With a little guidance, you will be making the most of your new operating system in no time. One of the biggest concerns for many people with new operating systems is privacy. This is not limited to technology however– we tend to be concerned about protecting out privacy in many arenas of life. As you set up your new operating system, this should be no exception. In order for you to freely and comfortably go through setting up and personalizing your OS, it is important to take the step we are about to discuss first. That way, you will have no worries in the privacy department moving forward.

When you are setting up your OS, there are two routes you can take to be sure your privacy is where you want it to be. As you go through the setup steps, you will come across a screen with the option to 'Use Express Settings'. If you want to be sure the settings on your PC or tablet reflect what you are comfortable with from the start, do not go the fast, easy route and select that option.

Instead, click on 'Customize settings' on the left of the screen. The alternative is to use the express settings and finish setup quickly. You can then make any adjustments you feel are necessary to those settings. None of the defaults from the express settings are irreversible; so do not live in fear of that. The settings menu on your PC or tablet running Windows 10 has a dedicated privacy section. Navigate your way to it and you will be able to customize every aspect until you are comfortable and satisfied.

Once you have opened the privacy section in the settings menu, you will notice a long list on the left side. All of these are categories under the header of privacy. That means you can set and customize those for things such as location, camera, contacts, messaging, and much more. It starts off with a tab titled 'General' in which you can toggle things on or off such as personalized advertising ID, SmartScreen filter, sending Microsoft your typing and writing data, and allowing browsers to understand your configured language. From the four options, the one most people seem to want to toggle off is the personalized advertising ID. This means you will see random ads in apps that have them rather than information being sent to tailor those ads to you.

All you need to do is go through every category on the privacy section and be sure everything is toggled on or off as you prefer. If any areas allow exceptions or require some other kind of setting (size, volume, etc.) you will easily be able to access those options from within that same menu. And once you have done that, it is time to get a feel for your new operating system!

Chapter Two: Personalize Your New OS

Aside from privacy settings, there are many ways you can personalize your new operating system. From the aesthetic of it to the time & date settings to the way the system actually runs, there is a plethora of options for you to explore! Of course, there are many ways and functions you can make use of these options, some of which are quite involved and require some knowledge of the deeper workings of operating systems. In this chapter, we will discuss and go through the most commonly adjusted areas.

The Look of Your OS

Prior to your upgrade, you probably had your system set up in a specific way that looked appealing to you. Various factors go into play there such as accent colors, lock screens, and layout. Even themes play a role in how your PC's or tablet's system will look. To get started on customizing your system for you and your needs, revisit the Settings menu and select the 'Personalization' tab. Under that tab, you will see the option to customize the background, colors, lock screen, themes, and start menu.

The background section is where you select and fit your wallpaper image. There is even an option to have a slideshow rather than one stationary image; it is as simple as selecting a slideshow folder as the background rather than just a photo. So if you have recently taken a trip, are an art fan, or simply can't make up your mind on one photo this is definitely an option to consider.

The colors section offers you the ability to pick an accent color for the Windows 10 operating system. What exactly is an accent color and where will it show up? An accent color is used to emphasize a specific area and this is exactly how it functions within Windows 10. The accent color will show up on the taskbar, Start menu & screen, and will be part of your window borders. There is the option for Windows to automatically pick an accent color based off your background image or, with 48 options, you can choose your own!

The first thing you see when you open up the Lock Screen section is an image preview of what your lock screen looks like. This comes in handy when deciding to keep the current one or when customizing it to be sure it looks like you want it to. The preview will be followed up with the background, detailed status, and quick status settings. Under background in the lock screen section, you can choose between the three options of Windows Spotlight, picture, or slideshow. Setting a picture or slide show as your lock screen may be self-explanatory, but the option for Windows Spotlight may be a lot less clear. If you select Windows spotlight, the lock screen will default to a Windows theme on your PC. As for the detailed and quick status information (think widgets or notification bars), you can select one for a detailed status and up to seven for the quick statuses.

The themes section primarily serves as a link to 'classic theme settings' where you will be able to customize your theme.

So that finally leads to the Start menu section. One of the most talked about new features of Windows 10 is the return of the Start menu with its own upgrades. And with that comes the chance to customize it to better suit your wants and needs. You can decide whether or not you want app and content suggestions to appear in the Start menu, if you want recently used programs displayed, if you'd like to be shown what apps were recently added, and customize what links go on the Start menu. You can even decide to keep the full-screen menu when in desktop mode on or off. Not only is this feature back, it is something you can make your own along with the rest of the options to personalize the look and feel of your new Windows 10 operating system.

Default Apps

Like with any operating system, certain files are automatically opened using certain apps by default. Similarly, there are some actions that will open an app by default as well. With Windows 10, you will find this function has been simplified for ease of use. After opening up the settings menu, navigate to system and select the default apps section. You will then see options for categories such as calendar, email, maps, and so on for which you can choose the default app. If you are pleased with the app the system has assigned, you do not need to do anything. If you would like to select a different app for a specific function, simply click on the icon of the app assigned and select from the options that pop up.

Taskbar

Windows 10 uses the familiarity of previous versions of the taskbar while adding unique and new features of its own, similar to the Start menu. The most basic and essential features have remained unchanged. By default, the taskbar is placed at the bottom of the screen but it can be moved to any side of the screen. It houses the Start button, buttons for pinned and running apps, and system notifications next to the clock. Items can still be pinned to the taskbar including applications and web sites.

So what is new or improved? To the right of the Start menu button you should notice two new controls. These are the Cortana search box and the Task View button, both of which can be removed (and resized for the Cortana search box) if you prefer not to have them on your taskbar. You can still use the Cortana feature by opening the start menu and use a keyboard shortcut (WinKey + Tab) for Task View without having them take up that extra space on your taskbar.

Additionally, there is now the Action Center which functions as a notification center in Windows 10. Especially useful for touch devices (such as tablets), is the ability to add quick actions such as screen rotation lock and access to the settings menu. Up to four tiles for quick actions can be selected from a longer variety of options. Another new feature comes when you are in desktop mode. You will notice all apps are displayed on the taskbar.

You can also configure the features of your taskbar simply by right clicking on an empty area of the taskbar and choosing from the available options. To set the configurations for taskbar, select properties and you will be able to make your changes and selections.

Tablet Mode

With the popularization of tablets and the influx of 2-in-1 tablet and PCs, it is important to note that Windows 10 has taken these users into consideration. The beauty of this operating system is that it works equally well on traditional PCs (desktops and laptops), tablets, and the newer 2-in-1 machines. So what helps it work so well across the board? Something Microsoft has introduced to machines running their software called Tablet Mode. Tablet mode optimizes Windows for touch screen devices. The following paragraphs will briefly touch on all the biggest differences you will notice right away after switching to Tablet Mode.

To start, everything will be full screen. Any open apps and windows will all change over to a special full screen mode. This means the desktop will be effectively hidden, although you can access it from File Explorer. The Start menu/screen will also become full screen. You will also notice how the app icons in the taskbar will disappear. It helps keep the aesthetic of the system clean and prevents you from accidentally opening an app by tapping it on the taskbar with your finger.

Many user interface elements will be a lot more touch-friendly as well. In addition to apps disappearing from the task bar, any icons remaining will be bigger and better spaced for touch screen optimization. There is also a back button similar to that of a Windows phones which allows you to navigate back through the system. A plus side to all of this is the device that you are using will work with a keyboard and a mouse even when you enable tablet mode. And you do not have to be using a touch screen device to enjoy many of these changes in tablet mode either! So if your personal preference runs more along these lines but you do not have a touch screen device, you can still make use of this new feature. You can decide how configure Tablet Mode on the system settings menu.

Favorite Settings and Shortcuts

With Windows 10, you can pin settings, settings groups, and even individual settings to Start. To pin Settings to Start, simply right click (tap and hold on touch screen device) and select 'Pin to Start' from the pop-up menu. If you want to pin a Settings group to Start, open the settings menu and right-click (tap and hold on touch screen device) the group of your choice, then select 'Pin to Start' from the pop-up menu. You can do the same for any individual setting. This will help to keep things at the tips of your fingers for greater ease of use.

Uninstalling Applications

Windows 10 makes it a bit easier to uninstall apps, except those that have been built in, than previous OS versions. Simply find the app's tile or icon either in Start or 'All Apps', right-click on it (tap and hold on touch screen device) and select 'Uninstall' from the pop-up menu!

Chapter 3: Cortana and Action Center

In chapter 2, you were taken through steps to personalize your new Windows 10 operating system. Of course there are many more things you can do to make it feel, look, and run as you prefer but the basics of it were covered in detail. Two great features, Cortana and Action Center, were mentioned and now this chapter will focus on detailing more information about them. Sure, you know how to toggle them and where to go to customize certain items pertaining to these two useful features but now you can know more extensively how these features can be utilized to best serve you.

Cortana – Setup & Features

So, what exactly is Cortana anyway? As Microsoft puts it, you can think of Cortana as your "clever new personal assistant". By using the upgraded Cortana, you can more easily locate and find things on your PC (such as apps and files), manage your calendar, and even track packages. A fun little addition to the program is that it has the capability to chat with you and even tell you a joke if you find yourself in need of entertainment or a good laugh. The more you use Cortana, the more tailored to you it will become. Here's the current catch with this new program: it only works in some regions of the world. It is currently available only in the United States, the UK, China, France, Italy, Germany, and Spain. It is of note to know more countries will be added as time goes on. Not to worry, if Cortana isn't available where you live (or you opt to leave it off), you can still use the old search function.

Cortana must be toggled on because it is switched off as a default setting. As mentioned earlier, the Search button is on the taskbar. Select it and complete the steps of the setup wizard. Cortana will need to collect information about you and store it in the cloud so that Microsoft can sync your preferences between multiple devices, there are also terms you will need to agree to for this function to work.

If you *do* have Cortana and decide to use it, you will want to configure it to work for you in order to get started. After switching it on, the next step in setting it up is deciding if you want it as a search box or button on your taskbar. Or, perhaps, you prefer not to have it on your taskbar at all. Either way, you can access Cortana via your keyboard or even using your voice. If you keep it on your taskbar, all you need to do is hit the WinKey on your keyboard to pull it up and you can start typing in your search or command. If you take it off your taskbar, simply hit the WinKey + C together and Cortana will come up so you can start typing. For voice activation, you simply say "Hey, Cortana". That's right, muttering those words as if you are greeting a friend, will pull up this helpful feature. All you need to do is enable the voice activation feature under the settings for Cortana and be sure your microphone works. If you would like, you can even set it up so that the feature *only* recognizes *your* voice! Finally, there is a Cortana tile on Start so this feature is everywhere and accessible – you can't miss it!

Then comes the actual configuration. Think of it as an introduction of sorts. In order for Cortana to best serve you and provide the most personalized search and help experience, the program needs to know more about you. So how does Cortana keep track of the info gathered about you in order to be tailored for your use? It stores all the information in its very own notebook. You can even take it upon yourself to add some information about yourself to the notebook. The notebook has different categories such as Eat & Drink, Events, Finance, Getting Around, Meetings & Reminders, and Movies & TV for you to input information in to and for the program to pick up information and store it as you use it more and more. Once you have set up and configured Cortana, you will find the feature useful and realize that it can send alerts (work schedule, flights, etc.), send reminders (meetings, events, etc.), recommend restaurants in the vicinity, and much more.

Cortana - Reminders

One of the best improvements made to Cortana since its debut is the ability to create reminders within it as a quick action. You can even set the reminder to be triggered by a time, location, or a person. What does this mean? If you want a time-based reminder, you can set it to go off at a specific time (for example at 9pm on a certain date). A good example of using this function is if you need to make a call or pay a bill. You can also set it to be recurring. For example, if you are taking a dance class every Wednesday at 8pm, Cortana can remind you each time that it is coming up. Finally, you can set approximate times. For example, you can have Cortana remind you to go to the post office the following afternoon.

Reminders triggered by location go off when you are at that particular place. For example, if you are going on a business trip to New York and the first thing you need to do is check-in to your hotel, you can ask Cortana to remind you to "check-in to my hotel when I get to New York." Once you arrive and Cortana detects your location, the reminder will go off! A reminder triggered by a person can be set so when that person text messages or calls you, Cortana will send that previously set reminder. It is a very useful feature with many options.

Action Center – Notifications

Windows already had the capability of the system and apps being able to notify users of important events when necessary. However, it was not until the release of the upgraded operating system Windows 10 that the functionality of the notification system has blossomed. The Action Center incorporates the old functions of the notifications and can now also be used to access and manage missed notifications. Windows 10 supports lock screen notifications and pop-up notifications for both apps and the system. This new Action Center can be seen as similar to the existing notification bars of Android and iOS systems. One thing that they have in common is that the Action Center's default visibility setting is set to be hidden, keeping record of those missed or ignored notifications.

So how can you bring up the Action Center if it is hidden? You can click on the icon (located on the system tray), swiping inward from the right edge of the screen on a touch screen device, or by hitting WinKey + A on your keyboard simultaneously.

Once you bring up the Action Center, another similarity to Android and iOS you will notice is that it not only houses missed and ignored notifications, it is also lined with Quick Action tiles at the bottom. What are these Quick Action tiles? They are frequently used and adjusted settings such as toggling Wi-Fi and Bluetooth on and off, adjusting screen brightness, switching on to airplane mode, and so on.

How do the actual notifications work in the Action Center and what can you do with them? To close a notification, just select the 'x' button at the right of it. This is useful if you have already seen it or it is one that is not important or relevant. If you want to clear *all* the accumulated notifications, select "Clear all" at the top of Action Center. To expand an individual notification to read more detail, select the 'v' icon located just below the 'x' to close it. If you do not want to clear the notification after reading the details provided upon expanding it, then tap the '^' to collapse it. If you want or need to respond to a notification, simply select it from the list of notifications in the Action Center. Doing this will trigger the related app and redirect to the item that triggered the notification so you can respond.

Of course, you can customize some notification settings. Go the Settings menu and under 'System', select 'Notifications & actions'. You will then see the areas you can configure. By default, the option to have the Action Center show tips about Windows is enabled. This means Windows will pop-up helpful tips about using the operating system. This can be especially useful when you first upgrade to Windows 10. Another option enabled by default is to "show app notifications". It determines if apps display pop-up notifications or not. The "show notifications on the lock screen" option is also enabled by default. Now, it is the option to "hide notifications while presenting" that is actually disabled as the default setting. What is it, exactly? If you enable it, this setting prevents Windows and apps from displaying any pop-up notifications when you are using PowerPoint or projecting the display to a second screen for presentations. This comes in handy if you are at work or school and do not wish to be disturbed during that time.

So is it possible to determine what apps send notifications or are all set by default to do so and you have no choice? Not at all! Like so many other areas of the new Windows 10, you can edit this configuration to suit your wants and needs. The "show notifications from these apps" area is where you decide and set which apps are allowed to display pop-up notifications to you. Now that we have covered notifications for the Action Center, we can go move on to information on Quick Actions.

Action Center – Quick Actions

This function is especially useful for touch screen devices such as Windows smart phones, tablets, and 2-in-1 machines. From the Action Center, you can quickly access frequently used or adjusted system settings using the quick action tiles. What are quick action tiles? They look pretty much exactly what they sound like: those familiar tiles from the newer Windows operating systems. These quick actions provide access to those frequently needed, used, or adjusted system settings just with one simple tap (or click on a non-touch device). By default, four quick action tiles are displayed in the action center. However, this area can be expanded to show more of them if needed.

Of course, Windows 10 allows you the freedom to configure which four quick action tiles appear when the quick action area is collapsed. Head over to the settings menu and go to the 'System' section. Select 'Notifications & actions' and you will see an area to select the four tiles for quick actions. There will already be four there set by default. Simply select one by tapping or clicking on it and a pop-up menu will appear so you can select a new tile.

So what are the available options for these useful, little tiles? To begin, you can choose to include a tile for 'All Settings'. This is handy if you find yourself constantly wanting or needing to adjust any settings on your device. The quick action tile makes that Settings menu is very quickly and easily accessible. You can also select quick action tiles for things like toggling on and off Wi-Fi, Bluetooth, Tablet mode, screen rotation lock, quiet hours, airplane mode, location services, and battery saver. You can also choose quick action tiles that will allow you to adjust screen brightness, open OneNote, launch VPN settings, or open the 'Connect' panel. Once you have selected the top four quick action tiles and gotten a feel for everything, you will find the new Action Center to be very useful!

Chapter 4: Mail and Calendar

With the predominant usage of email for everything from school to work to your personal life, it is important to have apps and settings that make everything efficient and clean. With the widespread popularity of online calendars and the use of tablets as daily planners, the same goes for the calendar on your device– whether it be a Windows smart phone, tablet, 2-in-1, or traditional PC (desktop or laptop).

Gmail and Google Calendar

One of the most popular search engines is Google and it is definitely a powerhouse when it comes to the internet. Many people use both Gmail and Google calendar for business and personal. It is no question of importance, then, to explore how to best work both of these in the new Windows 10. In this upgraded Microsoft operating system, both the Mail and Calendar apps directly support these services by Google. This makes integration a lot easier and efficient once it is all set up. So how do you configure these universal Mail and Calendar apps to work with Google's services of the same function?

Start by setting up your Google account in the app. It is important to note that setting up your Google account in one app, whether it be Mail or Calendar, will automatically connect it to and enable it in the other. If you have just upgraded and installed Windows 10 and it is your first time opening either Mail or Calendar, you can enter the information for your Google account while setting up and running the app for the first time. If you have already run the app once, you can add the information for your Google account to it by selecting the little settings gear located in the lower-left of the Mail or Calendar apps. Then select "Accounts" followed by "Add an Account". This will prompt the "Choose an Account" window to appear. Of course, select "Google" and then follow the steps as laid out in the setup wizard.

Once you have successfully done this, you can actually start configuring. There are default settings, of course, but with something like Mail & Calendars you are likely to have specific needs. Like setting up the Google account, any changes you make to the settings in Mail will be applied to Calendar and the same holds true the other way around. From the 'Change mailbox sync settings' under the 'Accounts' panel of the app you will be able to set how often Mail is updated, how often calendars sync, how often your contacts sync, and how much email to download to the app. You can even decide if you want your email synced at all. After all the initial set up, the Mail and Calendar apps are ready to use.

You will find there are handy quick actions in these apps too. If you are using a mouse, hover over an email message to display available actions such as archive, delete and flag. If you are using a touch screen device, swiping over the message toggles these quick actions. Swiping to the right will set (or take off) a flag. Swiping to the left will archive the message. However, even these actions can be configured under settings. As for the Calendar app, you can decide which display and trigger notifications.

Calendar App – A Closer Look

The Calendar app can be connected to multiple accounts, allowing you to manage work and personal schedules if need be. This surely comes in handy for a multitude of people. Here is the catch: the Calendar app only works with online accounts. Despite that, you will find the app to be very useful.

The Calendar app includes a collapsible menu toggled by the '≡' symbol. Just like you might have taken your time in the past perusing different schedulers and deciding whether you wanted weekly or monthly layouts, you can select a view for your calendar to suit your needs. The difference here is you can switch out views as needed. The Calendar app offers the standard views such as day, week, and month. It also offers a useful workweek view that may not be as standard on other devices, or even traditional paper planners. Finally, the Windows 10 Calendar app offers multi-day views as well. This means you can see 2, 3, 4, 5, or 6 days rather than selecting an entire week or workweek. How can you set this? By selecting the drop down next to the 'day' menu item. Even one step further in tailoring this to your needs is being able to configure what constitutes a workweek and even setting the first day of the week. This is especially useful since not everyone has a Monday through Friday job.

Another useful capability of this Calendar app is that it supports multiple accounts, as previously mentioned. This means you can sign in with your Microsoft account but you can also add calendars for accounts from Outlook, Google, and even iCloud. There are, of course, more options of accounts you can add. You can also add quite a bit of details to your events, including meetings, so you have everything you need right at your fingertips. Something to note is also that Calendar events are available on the lock screen and the Calendar app can be set as the detailed status notification for it.

Chapter 5: User Accounts, Security, Backup & Recovery

Aside from setting up more than one user account and taking care of privacy options, there is more that goes into the fold of user accounts and security. In this chapter, we will cover the key points for both of these to set your mind at ease and get everything flowing as smoothly as possible.

Microsoft Family – The New Parental Controls

One of the bigger concerns when it comes to user accounts comes down to parental controls. With a plethora of information, graphics, and websites in general out on the internet for anybody to access, it is no wonder this is a growing area of concern for parents. It is important to be sure children only have access to age appropriate websites and applications. Aside from the rebranding, a major change in the area of parental controls is the requirement for children to use a Microsoft account to sign in rather than a standard account (local to your PC or device). Microsoft Family allows settings to go across different devices when signed into the account. This makes things easier across the board in terms of parental controls. There is also an activity reporting notification system. The first time a child signs in to the account, this activity is reported. It is then reported again every 30 days. Something of importance is that the Store does not allow children to download content above their age rating. This means children deemed too young for something such as a violent game will not have access to it while signed in to his or her Microsoft account. It should go without saying, but it follows that adult websites are blocked. Furthermore, even Cortana is inaccessible to children under the age of thirteen.

It is possible to manage Microsoft Family in two ways: by signing in online via the Microsoft website or via the Settings menu on a PC. Being able to manage this remotely by signing in online is something that should prove to be quite useful for parents and caretakers. It is even possible to track activity over the last seven days across all Windows 10 and Windows 10 Mobile devices for that account. This will provide parents with a closer look as to what their children spend their time doing on the PC or Windows mobile devices.

Windows Hello

No, we are not greeting Windows. Windows Hello is the name of a new program set up in Microsoft's Windows 10 operating system for user sign-in as opposed to the traditional password. Though this requires specific technology and, as a result, may not apply to the bulk of the users out there it is still worth a mention. One of the features of this new program is facial recognition. This feature has been heralded as being extremely fast and, thus, speeding the sign-in process for the user. Windows Hello also makes use of fingerprint scan and even an iris scan.

Since these all require special technology, there is the high likelihood we will se an influx of new devices ready-made with the necessary equipment to make use of Windows Hello.

Backup & Recovery

It is no longer difficult to find the system backup and restore capabilities, something users of Windows in previous versions struggled with in the past. Windows 10 includes a variety of technologies to replicate and back up files on your PC. This allows a user to start over from scratch in the event of a hard drive failure. Hard drive failures are unwanted but often inevitable so it is always best to be as prepared as possible in the event it should happen. So what backup and recovery tools available in Windows 10?

The first is called 'File History'. This tool serves to automatically back up your most important files to a separate hard drive or network location. How does that differ from the backing up of files you are accustomed to doing? Well, in addition to backing up your most important files it also allows you to retrieve earlier versions of that file. Another feature is 'PC Reset'. It allows you to reset your PC back to the condition it was in the day you bought it. There is also an option to perform this reset wherein you can keep all your documents and data. This means you can also keep many of your installed apps, if you should want to. You can securely wipe the PC, something that would come in handy if you are either selling or gifting it. Then, you would not have to worry about anybody gaining access to your personal information and data previously stored on the hard drive.

With 'System image backup', you can restore your entire PC from a full system image backup. This same tool can be used to access files in any backups you made in previous versions of Windows (like Windows 7 or 8). The 'Windows Recovery Environment' tool allows you to boot the PC to perform various troubleshooting and system restore activities. This is done using various advanced recovery tools. This provides access to things like System Restore, System Image Recovery, Startup Repair, and a command prompt. You will find this tool can be quite useful if something goes wrong with your PC (as tends to happen from time to time).

Chapter 6: User Interface Basics

With Windows 10 launching across the board as the operating system for various Microsoft devices, the OS has a lot of changes and much to offer. That also extends to the area of the user interface. Whether the functions be new or updated versions of something that already existed in previous versions of Windows, this chapter will take you through important UI areas to understand them better and make the most of them.

Keyboard Shortcuts

Despite all the tiles, buttons, pins on taskbars and even Cortana available on Windows 10, sometimes the penchant to utilize keyboard shortcuts still wins out. And this is no surprise given you may be running a full screen program and want to pull something up quickly. Everyone has a preferred method of doing things and it never hurts to be well versed in the many options available to you. So how can you create keyboard shortcuts in Windows 10?

Start by selecting 'All apps' under the Start menu. Locate the app you want to create a keyboard shortcut for and then right click on it. Select the 'Open file location' option from the pop-up menu if it is available. If it is not, that means the app is a native app or from the Windows Store. This is where the next step differs. If the 'Open file location' option is not available, meaning it is a native Windows app, then you simply click and drag the app from the Start menu onto the desktop. This will create a desktop shortcut.

Right click on the newly created desktop shortcut and select 'Properties' from the menu that pops up. If the 'Open file location' option did appear and you selected it, you should then proceed to also select 'Properties'. This is where the steps that follow are the same for either type of app. Once the 'Properties' window opens, you will see a 'Shortcut' tab and then a section for 'Shortcut key'. All you have to do is enter the desired shortcut onto the blank line of text and then click 'Apply' once it has been set. After that you should be able to use your newly created keyboard shortcut! What is even more convenient about making your own rather than relying on a preset keyboard shortcut is you can create one that makes sense to *you* and, thus, will be much easier to remember.

Multiple Desktops

In this case, we are not referring to using more than one desktop PC at a time. Instead, this section refers to the use of multiple "virtual desktops" on one screen. This comes in handy for something like multitasking. Instead of having multiple windows open at once and having to sort through those, you can separate them onto different virtual desktops and navigate those instead. Many people use this as an organizational tool. For example, they keep their research on the browser on one desktop and the presentation on another. Another example is separating everything pertaining to multiple projects by virtual desktops as well. The uses for this feature are many. Unfortunately, this Windows 10 capability is still in need of some polishing. You cannot drag and drop programs between different screens, something many users would find extremely useful. Though less of a serious offence, you can't set a unique wallpaper for every individual virtual desktop. Perhaps the most limiting factor of this tool is the inability to jump quickly to a particular screen without having to cycle through all your open screens. This is clunky and time consuming, something far from ideal for such a neat feature.

Despite these limiting factors, it is still worth knowing how to use and navigate this capability. How do you go about adding a virtual desktop? It is actually rather simple. On the task bar you will see two overlapping rectangles. That is the 'Task View' button. Click on it to open 'Task View' and then click on 'New Desktop'. You can also open 'Task View' by hitting WinKey + Tab simultaneously and then select 'New desktop' from there. Once you already have two virtual desktops open and you want to open a third, fourth, or more, the 'Add a desktop' button will appear as a grey tile with a plus symbol. Of course, there is a keyboard shortcut to quickly open a new virtual desktop as well. Simply hold down WinKey + Ctrl + D simultaneously to do so.

Once you have two or more virtual desktops open, you will need to know how to switch between them to find and use what you need according to how you've sorted everything out. If you choose to use the keyboard shortcuts, this is where you need to cycle through all your open virtual desktops to get to the desired one. The keyboard shortcuts are WinKey + Ctrl + Left/Right arrow. If you do want to select a specific desktop, then you cannot do so using the keyboard shortcuts. You need to open 'Task View' and then click on the desired desktop.

We mentioned you cannot drag and drop windows from one desktop to another but that does not mean you cannot move windows between desktops at all. It just means it is not as simple as virtually moving them around. In order to do this, you must open up Task View first and then hover your mouse over the desktop housing the window you wish to move to another desktop. Right click on the window, select 'Move to' and the select the designated desktop. So it is not difficult, it is just not as quick and easy as dragging and dropping.

Finally, to close a virtual desktop just open up 'Task View' and hover your mouse over the desktop you want to close. Once a small 'x' appears on the upper right corner, click on it and the virtual desktop will be closed. Another option to close a virtual desktop is to use the keyboard shortcut WinKey + Ctrl + F4. This will serve to close out the desktop you are currently on; it will not bring up a menu to select a desktop to close.

Goodbye Charms Bar

If you were already a Windows user and were using Windows 8 prior to upgrading to the new Windows 10, you must be familiar with Charms bar (even if you did not know that was the name of it until now). What you will notice in Windows 10 now is the absence of said Charms Bar. So what was the Charms bar and where was it located? It appeared from the right side of the screen (by moving your mouse over it) and gave you access to prime settings. It also presented options to share, print and search from whatever current app you were using when you opened up the Charms bar.

It sounds like it was a rather indispensible tool providing it had quite a few uses but Windows did away with it anyway. So how can you go about making use of those same features if the tool is gone? That is precisely what will be covered in this section of the chapter.

If you want to access the full Settings screen in Windows 10, simply click the Start button. This will display the new Start menu from which you can click Settings to pull up that screen. It really is not complicated or time consuming, which is great considering the Charms bar is no longer available. Although the Settings menu may have a new look, it offers the same options as before and even more. As for other options accessible from the Settings bar, you can now find many of them on the 'System Tray'. The 'System Tray' is located on the lower right corner of the screen. There you will find access to things such as network, volume, and notifications.

System Tray

Just like in the previous versions of Windows, the 'System Tray' is customizable in Windows 10. The only difference now is where you must navigate to in order to configure the 'System Tray' as you would like it. In Windows 10, right click on the actual Taskbar and then select 'Properties' from the pop-up menu that appears. Then click the 'Customize' button followed by 'Select which icons appear on the taskbar'. You should be able to toggle an app to the 'on' position if you wish for it to permanently show on the right side of the taskbar. If you would like to, you also have the option to move items such as 'Network' and 'Volume' to the System Tray. You also have the option to remove those icons entirely.

Chapter 7: Cool Features

Many of the new and updated features in Windows 10 are very useful and exciting, that is for sure. All of the topics covered so far have been the most essential– from how your operating system looks to how it runs. We have covered big changes to be aware of, how to configure things, and where to find tools that have been moved. Those have been the basic and most used functions. Otherwise, they are functions many have wanted for years or the kind of thing that, once you discover it, you can't stop using it. Now we will cover a couple more cool, new features you can find in Windows 10 and should definitely check out. We are willing to bet you will find these features useful and, if you do not, you will at the very least find them interesting.

Writing on Web Pages

Have you ever been on a site researching something or just perusing leisurely and thought you wanted or needed to take note of something? More than likely this has occurred to you on more than one occasion. Windows 10 comes with its own browser called 'Microsoft Edge'. While it has quite a few new features such as a reading view and a fast, secure rendering engine, there is one that stands out the most– being able to draw, write on, and mark up web pages directly in the browser. Think of it essentially as having printed out the page and then marking it up in any way you want or need. You can even share the doodled web pages via email, through social networks, or save them to OneNote. In the upper right corner of the browser window, you will see a small icon that looks like a pen and a paper. Simply click on it for the web page to automatically refresh and introduce with it a specialized toolbar above the regular toolbar, with five icons: pen, highlighter, eraser, text, and clip. Click on the icon you would like to use and go crazy!

If you want something a little neater, you can type in comments as well. Just click on the text button and then click on the spot of the page where you would like to drop a pin. That pin will have a text box next to it in which you can type out your notes or comments. Just click on the pin to collapse it for a nice, clean look to the web page.

Once you are done marking up your web page and adding any comments you want, you will need to save it. You will see save and share icons on the right side of the tool bar containing the icons to mark up the web page. Simply click the save icon and a menu will pop up offering you three different options to save– OneNote, adding it to favorites, or adding it to your reading list. If you wish to share the web page, click on the share icon and select if you want to share the link or a screenshot before choosing what program to send it through.

Photos

Windows 10 comes with a photo app replete with different functions for the user. With the predominance of camera-equipped smartphones, more affordable digital cameras, and easily accessible (and extremely popular) social networking, people are documenting more and more of their every day– let alone special events– and needing a place to store all those photographs. So it should be of no surprise that integrating a useful and helpful photo app is something any operating system should strive to do. Instead of just being a place to store photos, this new default Photo app will organize your pictures by the date they were taken, create albums for you, provide a few basic but helpful editing tools to enhance images, and allow you to share pictures via email and upload them to social networks. It is definitely a lot more inclusive than just a photo dump, so to speak.

In the app you will notice two sections: collection and albums. Collection is all of your photos only grouped by the date taken. Microsoft did think ahead and realize people could have years' worth of photos on their PC or Windows device. So, you can click (or tap) on a specific date to quickly find the photos you are looking for rather than scrolling through a huge list or gallery. The albums section is just what it sounds like– it is your photos arranged by the "albums" Windows has created based off factors like dates and locations.

You can add a folder to the app by going to settings within the app and clicking (or tapping) the 'Add a folder' option under the 'Sources' section. Then just locate the folder you want to add, select, and click 'Add this folder to Pictures'. Simple as that! Additionally, you can toggle off the option to show OneDrive photos in your Photos app under settings as well. If you would like to edit a photo, just click (or tap) on the desired photo to open it up to full size. Then click the pencil icon and the editing platform will open up. You will find tools and options to enhance your image such as basic fixes, filters, light, color, and effects. What are basic fixes, exactly? This Photos app

characterizes basic fixes as image rotation, cropping, straightening, red-eye reduction,

and the retouching tool. Those are all pretty straight forward and definitely fit under the

basics category. Under basic fixes you will also find an 'enhance' button. This means

the app will automatically take and adjust what it thinks needs to be fixed in the image.

This can be anything from lighting and contrast to the sharpness of the image. This

might work well for some photos but be aware it is not a quick one-stop for every image,

every time. That is why the other options to manually adjust things such as brightness,

contrast, highlights, shadows, colors, saturation, and so on are available as well. Just

click (or tap) around until you have explored, gotten a feel for the controls, and soon you

will be pleased with the work you have done to enhance your photos!

Conclusion

Now that you have installed Windows 10 and gone through this book, you might be feeling like there is so much to get done. And while you may be right, that is not a bad thing. It is exciting! You will learn, explore, and set up the operating system to best match your wants and needs. Considering how big a role traditional PCs (desktops and laptops), tablets, 2-in-1 machines, and smartphones play in our everyday lives, it is important to have an efficient operating system and be comfortable with it.

With the release of Windows 10, there is no need to panic about favorite features disappearing, things moving, or updates being made. After carefully reading through everything laid out in detail in this book, you should have a basic grasp of the most important functions offered by your new operating system. You should also be more aware of how you can best make use of it. All it takes is some time to read and a little bit of exploration to really get the hang of things. And once you do that, you will find you are smooth sailing faster than you thought you would! You will even likely make some discoveries of your own and feel more comfortable to see them through!